BOYS' TOYS

BIKES

SOURCEBOOKS, INC.
NAPERVILLE, ILLINOIS

Copyright © 2000 Unanimous Ltd
Cover design © WDA

Designer: WDA
Editor: Alison Moss
Researcher: Suzie Green

All rights reserved. No part of this book may be reproduced in any form or by any electronic or mechanical means including information storage and retrieval systems–except in the case of brief quotations embodied in critical articles or reviews–without permission in writing from its publisher, Sourcebooks.

Although effort has been made to trace all present copyright owners of text extracts, apologies are offered in advance for any unintentional omissions or neglect. The publishers will be happy to insert appropriate acknowledgments to companies and individuals in subsequent editions.

Sourcebooks, Inc.
P.O. Box 4410, Naperville, Illinois 60567-4410

(630) 961-3900
FAX: (630) 961-2168

Printed and bound in Hong Kong

MQ 10 9 8 7 6 5 4 3 2 1

ISBN: 1-57071-602-1

INTRODUCTION

Like the motor car, bikes have the ability to enthral the entire male species, from the earliest bone shakers through the romantic monsters of the golden age to the most up-to-date super bikes of the modern age.

Motor bikes have an appeal all of their own. Every young man owns one, or wants to. A small scooter with as much power as a hairdryer is often his first form of transport. Then as family and responsibility take priority, bikes are put to one side, like so many "silly" and childish things, to make way for reliable cars capable of carrying kids and groceries. But once the children have flown the coop, the urge to own a motor bike again takes precedent, and the battle to own a modern super bike or sports car is fought (with the gloves off) in living rooms across the world.

Why do bikes have such a hold over men of all ages? The speed for certain. The sense of freedom for sure. Flying along roads on two wheels, pulling the odd wheelie is a thrill comparable to no other. Dodging between cars as they stand hood to bumper on the parking lots that are our modern highways gives a man a feeling of superiority that a million dollars could not deliver. And of course, there's the tinkering: fixing and cleaning the engine of a power bike on the driveway where everyone can see, is guaranteed to draw many admiring glances.

In the early days there were the European bikes: powerful, sleek, and demanding. With names such as Rudge, Norton, and Triumph these bikes ruled the roads and the racetracks. Alongside these were the two great American biking names. First the Indian—a legend—a bike which was a major contributor to the success of the American Infantry in two World Wars, as messengers hurtled from trench to trench.

Then came the greatest bike of them all—the Harley Davidson—quite simply known as a Harley. What other bike can still capture the heart of the world after 80 years?

But there are also so many other bikes that fill men with joy. The modern Japanese motorcycles, while once derided, have now cut a niche of their own. Sleek, immensely powerful, and faster than a bullet from a gun, what man can possibly resist?

Within the pages of this book you will find images of all the greatest bikes, some standing like gods to be admired, others thick in the chase on the speedway. Paired with quotations, they capture the beauty and synergy of man and machine, the leathers, the chrome, the wheels, the speed, and the sheer excitement.

So climb aboard, hold on tight, and enjoy.

What you have is an engine that vibrates—shakes. Blurs mirrors and tingles hands and puts toes to sleep and rattles parts loose.

MV Agusta

THE IMPULSES FLOW BACK THROUGH HANDLEBARS, FOOTPEGS, AND SADDLE.

This is a 100% He-man Crimson-bleed Trial!

THEY WERE BRAVE MEN IN THOSE DAYS WITH MACHINES TO MATCH.

Indian Chief

Panther motorcycle

WHEN YOU SPOT A BIKE, FIRST FIND OUT WHAT MAKE IT IS.

The battle of Waterloo was won on the playing fields of Eton.

Evel Knievel

22

TRIALS ARE TESTS OF SKILL AND BIKE CONTROL OVER A VERY HAZARDOUS COURSE.

FOR A MECHANIC ON RACE WEEKEND,

HANDS ARE NEVER IDLE.

27

BEARDS AND HARLEY DAVIDSONS GO TOGETHER LIKE BASEBALL AND HOTDOGS.

Honda motorcycle

It must be the mystic thing or something but [I] ain't never seen an ugly looking chick on the back of a Harley.

Jealousy is the only vice that gives no pleasure.

Non riders always find this hard to believe
but you can control the throttle,
the front brake and the turn signal
with one hand, at once, while both feet
and your left hand are also engaged.

A GOOD SEAT IS AS IMPORTANT AS A GOOD ENGINE.

A MOTORCYCLE CAN'T BE COWLED IN SHEET METAL. THE ENGINE MUST LOOK LIKE AN ENGINE; A GOOD PORTION OF THE TUBE FRAMING MUST BE VISIBLE; THE WHEELS SHOULD BE OPEN. ALL COMPONENTS MUST BE IN THEIR PROPER PLACE.

AJS motorcycle

Is that a scratch?

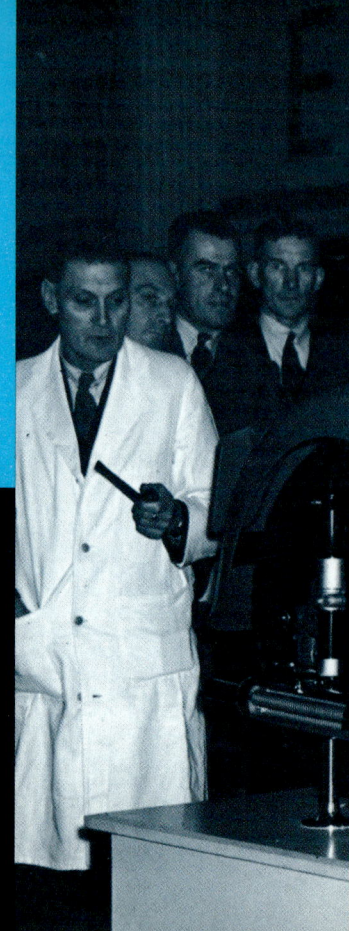

40

To many the image of the motorcycle is somewhat akin to that of a band of outlaws.

A BIKE MAKES YOU FEEL YOU COULD'VE BEEN SOMEONE.

48

The thrill of the chase...

51

The roar grew louder until the motorcycles blasted down.

52

To thy speed add wings.

SURROUNDED BY RUSHING WIND AND ENGINE'S MECHANICAL THRASHING,

75cc Moto Guizzi

THE RIDER SPEAKS A BODY LANGUAGE WITH HIS MACHINE AND THE ROAD BELOW.

I MUST HAVE BEEN CRAZY, THERE I WAS, A MARRIED MAN OF 40, WITH A FAMILY, RIDING LIKE A MADMAN.

YES, RIDERS, IT USED TO TAKE GUTS, GRISTLE, AND A GOOD RAIN SUIT TO SHOW UP ON A BIKE...IN MARCH.

AFTER EVERY SPLASH I WAS DELIGHTED TO FIND MYSELF PASSING FIELDS FULL OF EXHAUSTED HUMANITY PUSHING OR KICKING LIFELESS MOTORCYCLES.

**YOU CAN'T AFFORD TO MISS IT.
MAKE IT YOUR MOUNT IN 1924.**

Rudge motorcycle

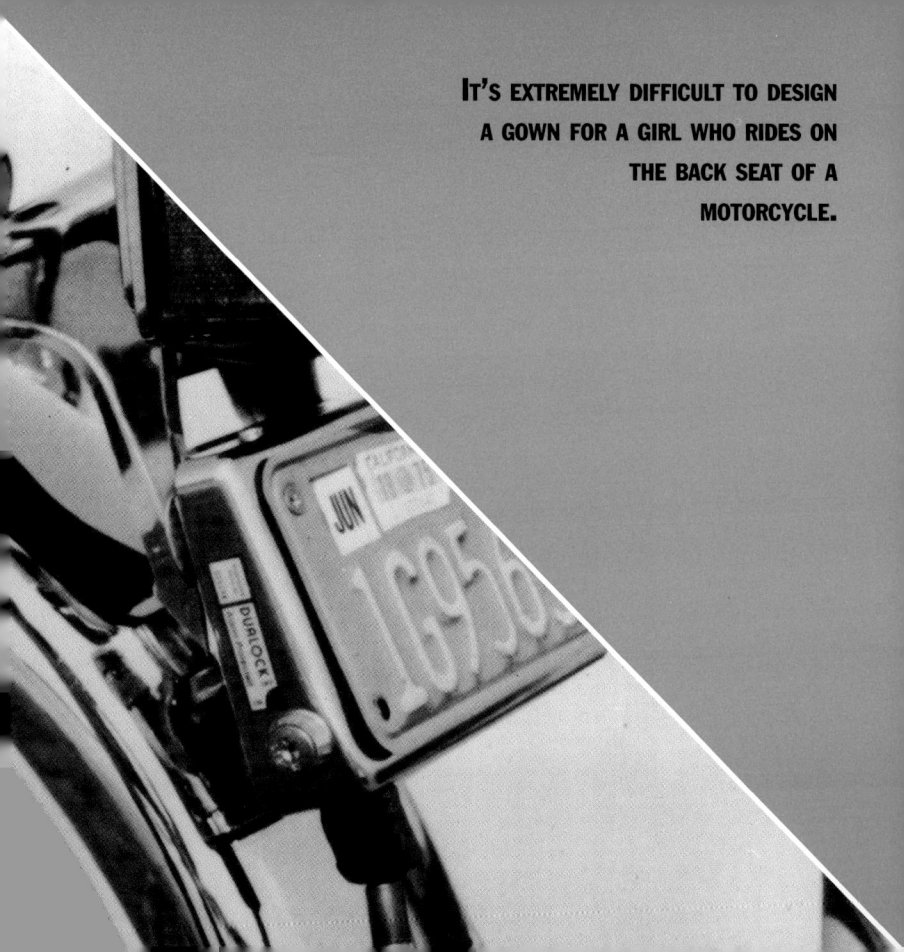

IT'S EXTREMELY DIFFICULT TO DESIGN A GOWN FOR A GIRL WHO RIDES ON THE BACK SEAT OF A MOTORCYCLE.

The bike is a strange creature, covered all over in dials and lights and levers.

Does that mean you face discomfort in the saddle?—Not a bit of it! In fact you can depend on absolute comfort all the time you are astride...

We whizz through the flat open land, not a car anywhere, hardly a tree, but the road is smooth and clear.

THE MOTORCYCLE EXUDED A MACHINE-LIKE QUALITY.

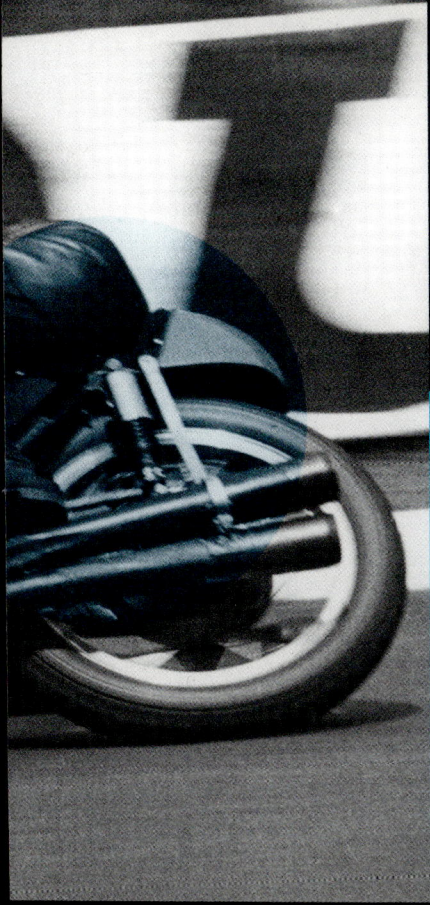

There are no speed limits on the road to success.

Act on impulse.

LIFE IS LIKE A BIKE.
MOST OF US HAVE GEARS
WE NEVER USE.

Coventry Eagle

THE MOTORCYCLIST WALKS AROUND HIS BIKE, PUSHING AND PULLING ON LEVERS AND PEDALS, WATCHING THE MECHANISMS OPERATE.

Commander motorcycle

85

MOTORCYCLES, NO MATTER HOW MODERN, ALWAYS APPEAR

AS ASSEMBLAGES OF SEPARATE PARTS.

And the talk: motorcycle racing, food, music, motorcycle racing, traffic, the lack of a really good fifty-cent drive-in hamburger, motorcycle racing, weather, last year's trip over the same route to the same place, the preparation of the machines, motorcycle racing.

Courage is almost a contradiction in terms. It means a strong desire to live taking the form of a readiness to die.

SIDECARS, OR MORE PROPERLY TERMED COMBINATIONS, ARE MACHINES APART FROM THE REST. THEY DON'T ACT LIKE FOUR WHEELERS AND THEY SURE DON'T ACT LIKE BIKES.

You can see my house from here.

Motorcycling Imps Display Team

80cc K11 sports bike

Enthusiasts knew why motorcycling wouldn't disappear. And the wind-in-your-hair, bugs-in-the-teeth rubbish has little to do with it.

Honda Chopper

There are countless ways to decorate your Vespa—with, for example, mirrors and flaps.

Gilera

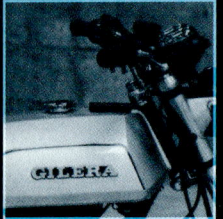

Rudge Ulster

THE FRAME IS A WORK OF ART.

PICTURE CREDITS

All images Hulton Getty Picture Collection

Page 8/9: Motorcycle at a show in Olympia, London, 1927.

Page 10/11: An MV Agusta motor bike at Brands Hatch, Surrey, circa 1965.

Page 12/13: Hairpin bend during a motorcross scrambling race at Suffolk County Club in Chatham, New York, circa 1955.

Page 14/15: Close up of the engine of a "new" motorcycle, 1948.

Page 16/17: Indian motorcycle, circa 1930.

Page 18/19: Children admiring a Panther motorcycle at a motorcycle show, 1960.

Page 20/21: Group of Eton schoolboys riding a motorcycle in an empty field, 1966.

Page 22/23: Stuntman Evel Knievel jumping over 13 buses at Wembley Stadium, London, 1975.

Page 24/25: Motorcyclist Sam Parriot performing one of his famous falls at the San Diego Motorcycle Hillclimb, 1926.

Page 26/27: World speedway champion Barry Briggs repairs his motorcycle in the pits at Wembley Stadium, London, 1958.

Page 28/29: Harley Davidson, 1979.

Page 30/31: Three members of the Cycle Sluts, London, 1976.

Page 32/33: British motorcycle racer Barry Sheene in action, circa 1980.

Page 34/35: Speedway riders on the track at Wembley Stadium, London, 1950.

Page 36/37: Tommy Price of the Wembley Lions team and winner of he 1949 World Speedway Championship has his name painted on the mud-guard of his motorcycle, 1950.

Page 38/39: An AJS 3.49hp motorcycle at the Motor Cycle Show at Olympia, London, 193.

Page 40/41: Sunbeam 500cc motorcycle at the Motor Cycle Show at Earl's Court, London, 1948.

Page 42/43: Norton motorcycle, 1954.

Page 44/45: The Devil's Henchmen motorcycle gang, 1971.

Page 46/47: Marlon Brando in a scene from the film "The Wild One," 1954.

Page 48/49: Staff Sergeant Monty Young with his boxer Fritz in Oceanside, California, 1961.

Page 50/51: Traffic cops from the LAPD on patrol, Los Angeles, circa 1975.

Page 52/53: Motorcross scrambling race at the Suffolk County Motor Club in Chatham, New York, circa 1955.

Page 54/55: Gary Hocking MBE on the Augusta Bridge, during the Senior Isle of Man TT Race, circa 1945.

Page 56/57: Italian motorcyclist Raffaele Alberti on his 75cc Moto Guzzi during his successful attempt at the world motorcycle speed record, 1949.

Page 58/59: Stunt motorcyclist Bill Deegan drives his motorcycle through a wall of blazing straw at Paddock Wood fete, Kent, 1964.

Page 60/61: Motorcyclist Tommy Price, 1950.

Page 62/63: Young team mates assist each other in a motorcycle scramble, circa 1955.

Page 64/65: The engine of a Rudge motorcycle at a BMCRC meeting at Brooklands, 1914.

Page 66/67: Honda motorcycle, 1975.

Page 68/69: Chopper motorcycle at the Motor Cycle Show, Earl's Court, London, 1977.

Page 70/71: Triumph Bonneville, 1979.

Page 72/73: Motorcyclist at the Eltham Motor Club in London, 1940.

Page 74/75: Irish motorcycling champion Stanley Woods, riding a Norton, on the track during the Junior Tourist Trophy Race on the Isle of Man, 1936.

Page 76/77: Derek Minter on his way to winning the 250cc TT event on the Isle of Man, circa 1962.

Page 78/79: Honda CB 900-FZ 5-speed sports bike at the International Motor Cycle Show, Earl's Court, London, 1978.

Page 80/81: The power unit of a Coventry Eagle on display at the Motor Cycle Show, Olympia, London, 1927.

Page 82/83: A Commander motor bike, 1953.

Page 84/85: An American teenager polishes his motorcycle, circa 1956.

Page 86/87: original caption unavailable.

Page 88/89: Riders chatting next to a BSA motor bike at Lenham, Kent, 1960.

Page 90/91: Rider on the track during the Tourist Trophy Race on the Isle of Man, 1936.

Page 92/93: A. H. Horton on his Norton during the Crystal Palace Vase race for motorcycles and sidecars, 1937.

Page 94/95: The Motorcyling Imps Display Team in action, 1977.

Page 96/97: Suzuki 80cc K11 sports bike.

Page 98/99: Merseybeat band The Undertakers, 1964.

Page 100/101: A "Rocker" arrives at Wembley Rock 'n' Roll festival on his Honda Chopper motorcycle, 1972.

Page 102/103: Gina Lollobrigada attends the Great Film Garden Party at Morden Hall Park in Surrey on a Vespa motor scooter, 1952.

Page 104/105: Gilera bike.

Page 106/107: Rudge Ulster motorcycle on view at the annual Motor Cycle Show, Olympia, London, 1935.

ATTRIBUTIONS

Page 8/9: Allen Girdler.

Page 10/11: Phil Schilling.

Page 12/13: Ixion's summary of the Scott Trial, 1927.

Page 16/17: Allen Girdler.

Page 18/19: David Minton.

Page 20/21: Arthur Wellesley, Duke of Wellington (attrib.).

Page 22/23: Anon.

Page 24/25: David Minton.

Page 26/27: Phil Schilling.

Page 28/29: Gerald Foster.

Page 30/31: Gerald Foster.

Page 32/33: Anon.

Page 34/35: Allan Girdler.

Page 36/37: Anon.

Page 38/39: Phil Schilling.

Page 40/41: Anon.

Page 44/45: Gerald Foster.

Page 46/47: Anon.

Page 48/49: Anon.

Page 50/51: Anon.

Page 52/53: Yves Lavigne.

Page 54/55: John Milton.

Page 56/57: Phil Schilling.

Page 58/59: Freddie Frith.

Page 60/61: David Wright.

Page 62/63: Harold Wood.

Page 64/65: Ariel the Dual Victor ad.

Page 66/67: Anon.

Page 68/69: Loren Robb.

Page 70/71: C. Edmund & Co. ad (1920).

Page 72/73: Robert M. Pirsig.

Page 74/75: Phil Schilling.

Page 76/77: Anon.

Page 78/79: Anon.

Page 80/81: Anon.

Page 82/83: Phil Schilling.

Page 84/85: Phil Schilling.

Page 86/87: Phil Schilling.

Page 88/89: Phil Schilling.

Page 90/91: G. K. Chesterton.

Page 92/93: Allan Girdler.

Page 94/95: Anon.

Page 98/99: Charles Udall.
Page 100/101: Phil Schilling.
Page 102/103: Andrea & David Sparrow.
Page 106/107: Sporting Cycle 1967.

Excerpted material by Allan Girdler used with permission from the book *Harley Davidson: American Motorcycle* by Allan Girdler. Published by MBI Publishing Company. © Allan Girdler, 1992.

Excerpted material by Robert M. Pirsig used with permission from the book *Zen and the Art of Motorcycle Maintenance* by Robert M. Pirsig, published in 1974 by Bodley Head.

Excerpted material by Phil Schilling from *The Motorcycle World* by Phil Schilling, A Ridge Press Book. published in 1974 by Hamlyn.

Excerpted material by Gerald Foster from *Cult of the Harley Davidson* by Gerald Foster, published in 1982 by Osprey Automotive.

Excerpted material by David Minton from *Cars, Motorbikes and Planes Handbook*, published in 1980 by Usborn Publishing.

Excerpted material by David Wright from the book *Harley Davidson Motor Company* by David Wright, 1983.

Excerpted material by Andrea & David Sparrow from *The Colour Vespa* by Andrea & David Sparrow, published in 1995 by Veloce.

Excerpted material by Yves Lavigne from *Hell's Angels: Into the Abyss* by Yves Lavigne, published in 1996 by HarperCollins.

Excerpted material by Loren Robb from *Bikes* by Loren Robb, published by Whitcoulis.